Norihiro Yagi won the 32nd Akatsuka Award for his debut work, *UNDEADMAN*, which appeared in *Monthly Shonen Jump* magazine and produced two sequels. His first serialized manga was his comedy *Angel Densetsu* (Angel Legend), which appeared in *Monthly Shonen Jump* from 1992 to 2000. His epic saga, *Claymore*, is running in *Monthly Jump Square* magazine.

In his spare time, Yagi enjoys things like the Japanese comedic duo Downtown, martial arts, games, driving, and hard rock music, but he doesn't consider these actual hobbies.

CLAYMORE VOL. 21
SHONEN JUMP ADVANCED Manga Edition

STORY AND ART BY
NORIHIRO YAGI

English Adaptation & Translation/John Werry
Touch-up Art & Lettering/Sabrina Heep
Design/Amy Martin
Editor/Megan Bates

Printed in the U.S.A.

Published by VIZ Media, LLC
P.O. Box 77010
San Francisco, CA 94107

10 9 8 7 6 5 4 3 2 1
First printing, November 2012

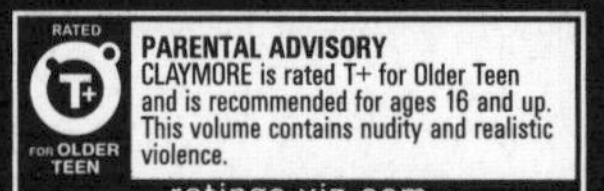

SHONEN JUMP ADVANCED Manga Edition

クレイモア

Claymore

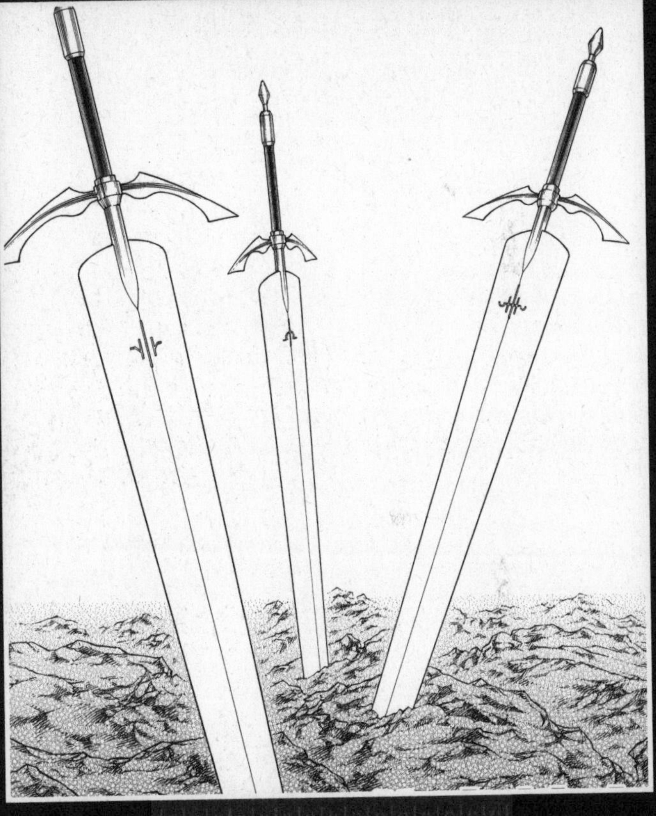

Vol. 21

Corpse of the Witch

Story and Art by Norihiro Yagi

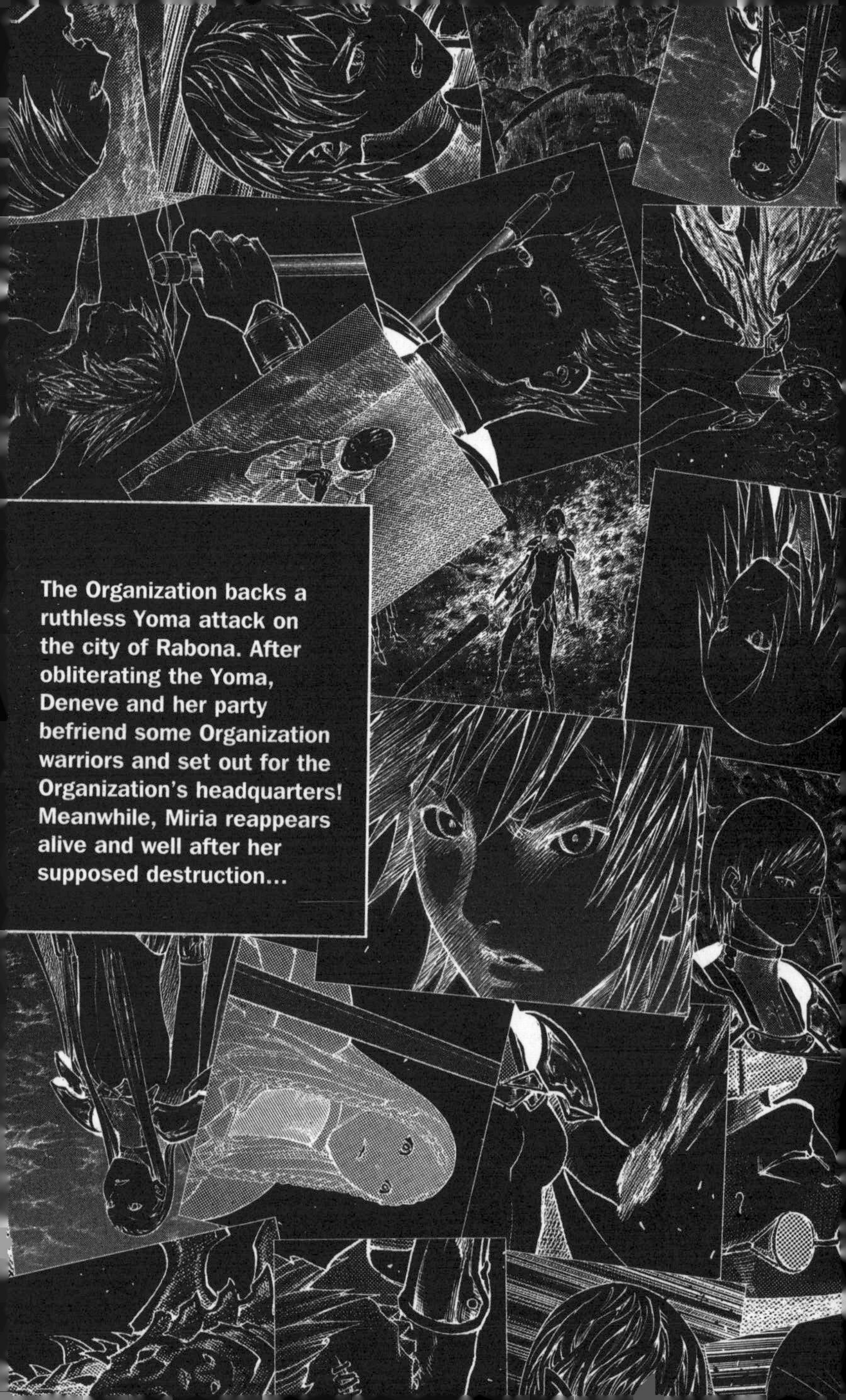
The Organization backs a ruthless Yoma attack on the city of Rabona. After obliterating the Yoma, Deneve and her party befriend some Organization warriors and set out for the Organization's headquarters! Meanwhile, Miria reappears alive and well after her supposed destruction...

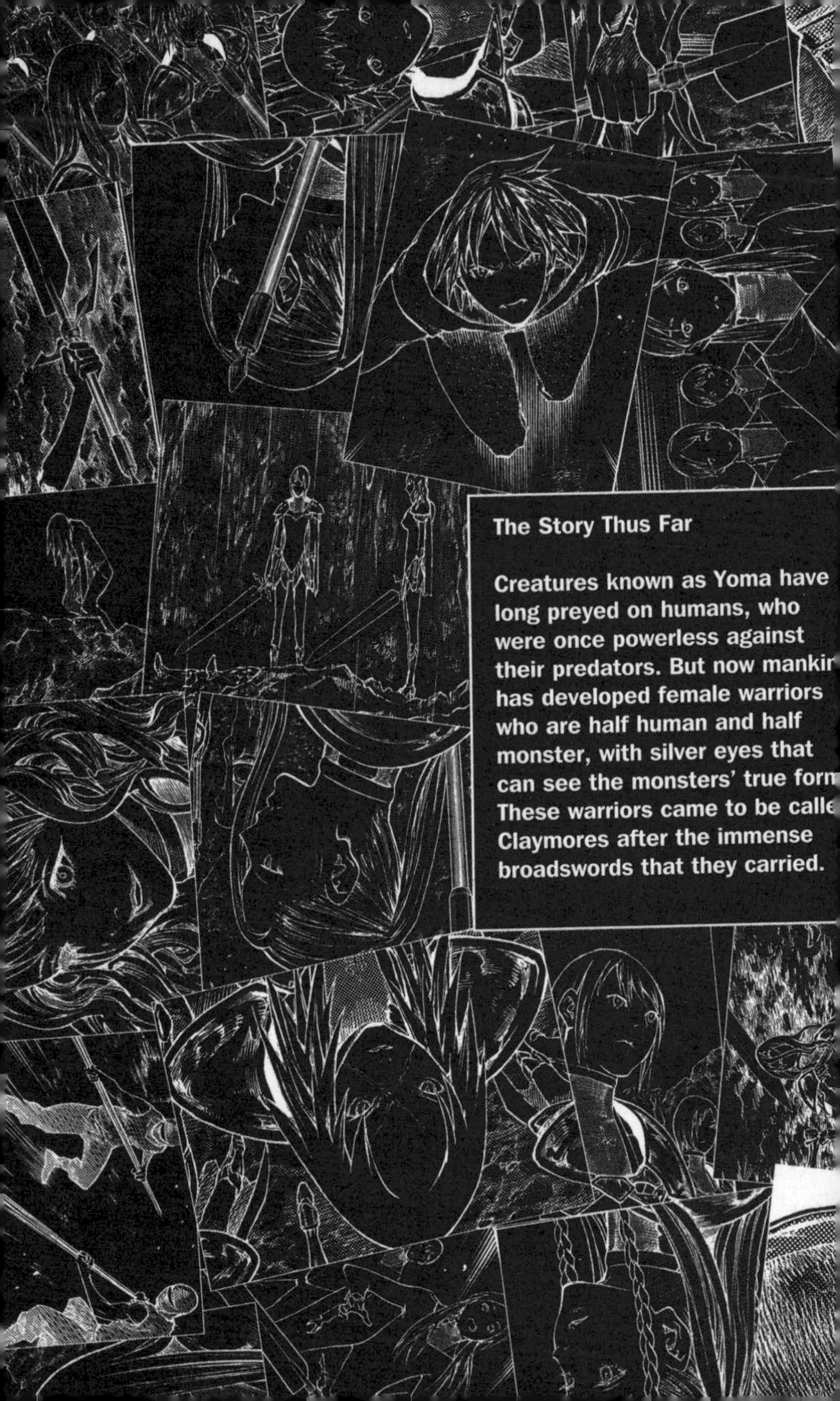
The Story Thus Far
Creatures known as Yoma have long preyed on humans, who were once powerless against their predators. But now mankin
has developed female warriors who are half human and half monster, with silver eyes that can see the monsters' true form
These warriors came to be calle
Claymores after the immense broadswords that they carried.

Claymore

クレイモア

Vol. 21

CONTENTS

SCENE 114: CORPSE OF THE WITCH, PART 1

SCENE 114: CORPSE OF THE WITCH, PART 1

GA
SHA

NUMBER 3, AUDREY...
NUMBER 5, RACHEL...
NUMBER 9, NINA...

NUMBER 7, ANASTASIA... NUMBER 8, DIETRICH...
...AND NUMBER 4, MIATA.

EXCEPT FOR NUMBER 6, RENÉE, WHO HAS DISAP-PEARED...
...ALL SINGLE DIGITS HAVE JOINED THE ENEMY.

READ THIS WAY

HOW'S YOUR LEFT ARM?
!
I FOCUSED ON HEALING THAT, SO UNFORTUNATELY YOU'VE STILL GOT SCARS.

AS LONG AS I CAN MOVE, IT'S ALL RIGHT.
I'M GRATEFUL JUST TO BE ALIVE.

HEH.
YOU'RE TOO SOFT.
YOU CAME TO CRUSH THE ORGANI-ZATION...
...WITHOUT KILLING ANY WARRIORS.
THAT'S A FATAL GOAL FOR A WAR-RIOR.
IT'S A MIRACLE YOU'RE STILL ALIVE.

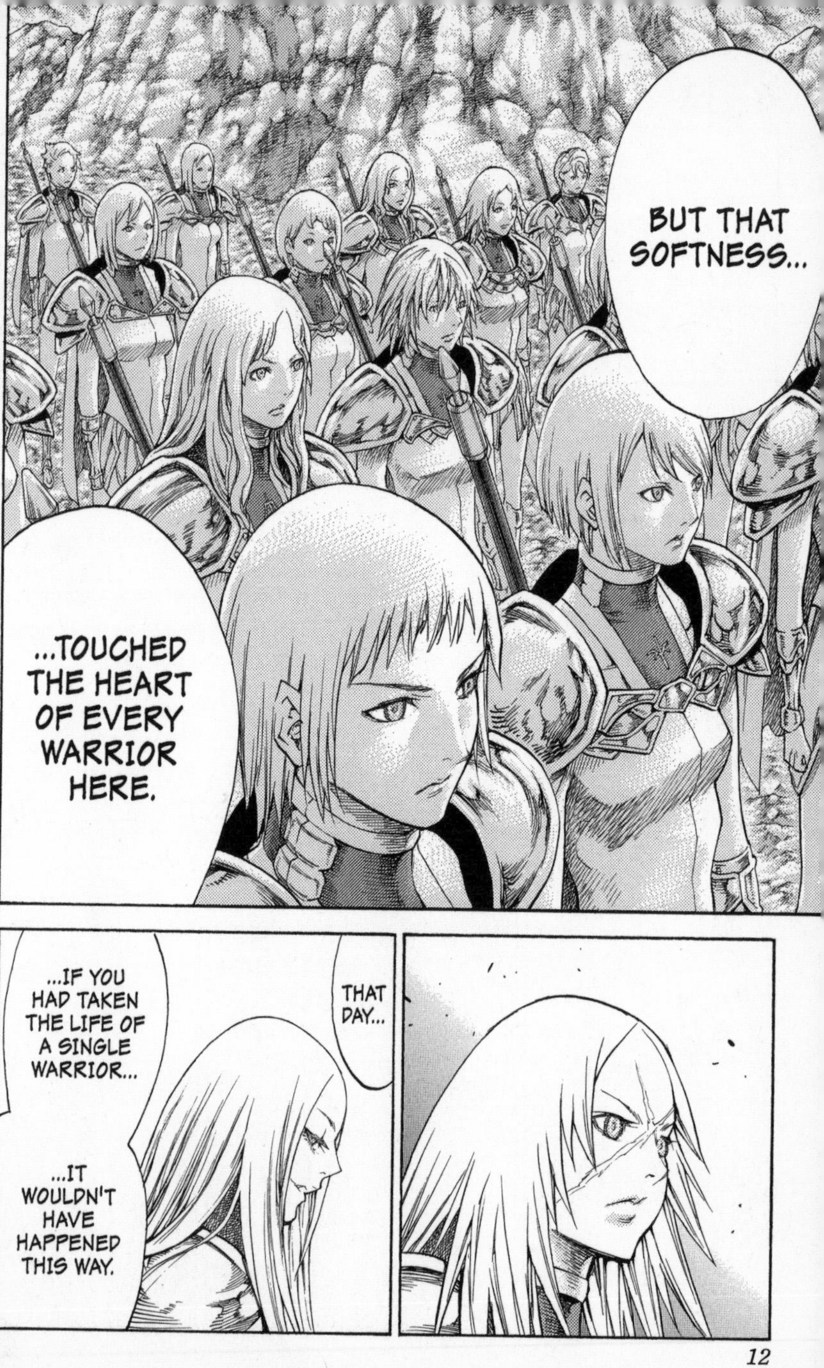

BUT THAT SOFTNESS...

...TOUCHED THE HEART OF EVERY WARRIOR HERE.

READ THIS WAY

BUT YOU SHOULD KNOW...
...THAT I HAVEN'T ACCEPTED YOU YET.

I'M JUST GOING ALONG WITH AUDREY.
NEVER FORGET THAT SHE HAD MERCY ON YOU.

I KNOW.
IF SHE HAD ATTACKED SERIOUSLY...
...I WOULDN'T HAVE BEATEN HER SO EASILY.

BUT, RACHEL...
...YOU *WERE* SERIOUSLY BEATEN.
FEH!
SHUT UP!
NINA...
WHAT OF NUMBER 10, RAFUTERA?

SHE'S STILL AT HEAD-QUARTERS.
IT SEEMS THAT AS A WARRIOR SHE WALKS A DIFFERENT PATH.

SHE IS THE ONLY WARRIOR WITH ANTI-WARRIOR TRAINING.
SHE REALLY DID TRY TO KILL YOU. WHAT SHOULD WE DO?

I WON'T KILL WAR-RIORS ...
...WHAT-EVER HER POSITION.
I WILL NOT CHANGE THAT.

THAT'S WHAT ...
...I THOUGHT YOU'D SAY.

GIVE US YOUR ORDERS, PHANTOM MIRIA.
EVERY WARRIOR HERE WILL FOLLOW YOU.

READ
THIS
WAY

GASHA

TAKE UP YOUR SWORDS.
A

ZA
TOGETHER, WE WILL...
...MAKE THIS DAY THE ORGANIZATION'S LAST!

EXCEPT FOR NUMBER 10, ALL THE WARRIORS HAVE BROKEN AWAY...

...AND NOW THEY ADVANCE ON THE ORGANIZATION!

READ THIS WAY

YOU ONLY EXIST IN ORDER TO COUNTER WARRIORS WHO REBEL.

WHY WOULD YOU JOIN THEM?

DO NOT HOLD BACK.

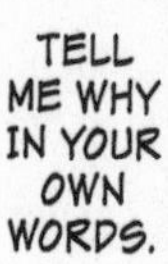
TELL ME WHY IN YOUR OWN WORDS.

THE WARRIOR THAT DAY...

...WAS MIGHTY, BUT FRAGILE.

!

THE WARRIORS THERE DISPLAYED MANY EMOTIONS.

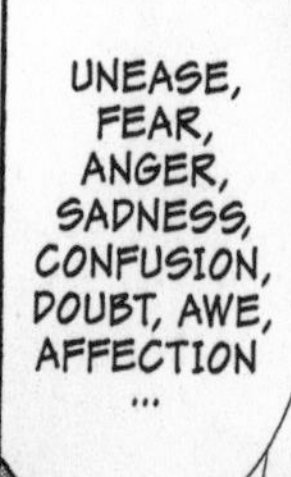
UNEASE, FEAR, ANGER, SADNESS, CONFUSION, DOUBT, AWE, AFFECTION ...

READ THIS WAY

ALTHOUGH WE ARE HALF DEMON, IN OUR HEARTS WE ARE MOSTLY HUMAN.
FOR THAT REASON, WHEN A WARRIOR SEES THE SUFFERING OF COMRADES SHE TRAINED AND FOUGHT WITH...
...SHE GROWS ANGRY AS IF SHE HERSELF WERE SUFFERING. AND WHEN SHE LOSES ONE OF HER FELLOW WARRIORS, SHE GRIEVES AS FOR A FRIEND.

WHEN THAT LONE WARRIOR CAME, IN A SINGLE INSTANT SHE AWAKENED WITHIN US STRENGTH AND WEAKNESS, HOPE AND DISAPPOINTMENT.
EVERYONE PRESENT WAS MOVED BY A SINGLE WILL TO REFRAIN FROM KILLING HER.

I AM SORRY...

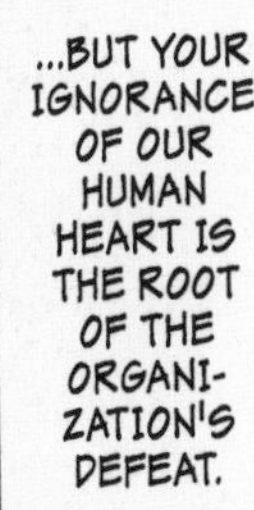
...BUT YOUR IGNORANCE OF OUR HUMAN HEART IS THE ROOT OF THE ORGANIZATION'S DEFEAT.

GASHU

DOS
HAAA

THIS IS WHAT COMES OF OUR ANTI-WARRIOR TRAINING.
NEXT TIME, WE MUST CRUSH THE VERY SOURCE OF THE SPIRIT.

HOW SOON ...
...WILL DAE BE READY?

WE ARE ENCOUR-AGING HIM TO MAKE HASTE...
...BUT HE WILL NOT BE FINISHED FOR A FEW MORE HOURS.

A...
...FEW HOURS ...

LOOSE THEM.
!
ALL OF THEM THAT THE ORGANIZATION HAS LEFT.
HOLD NOT A SINGLE ONE BACK.

BUT...
...WITHOUT A SPECIFIC TARGET...
...THEY WILL JUST RAMPAGE BLINDLY.

I DON'T CARE.
AT LEAST THEY'LL BUY TIME.

...
UH...

TELL EVERYONE IN THE ORGANIZATION...

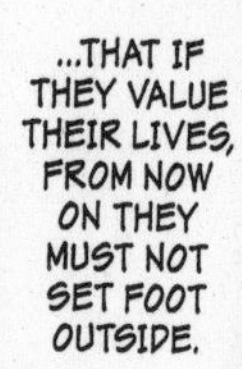
...THAT IF THEY VALUE THEIR LIVES, FROM NOW ON THEY MUST NOT SET FOOT OUTSIDE.

READ THIS WAY

GOOM

!

GOOM
GOOM
GOOM

WHAT'S THAT?
THAT SOUND...

IT...
... SOUNDS LIKE A HEAVY DOOR OPENING.

!
?!

WHAT'RE THOSE?
WAR-RIORS ...?
NO, I DON'T SENSE ...
...ANY YOMA ENERGY...

GEH
GEH
SHIVER
GEH

GAAAH

!!
HIGHER NUMBERS, PROTECT THE LOWER NUMBERS!
THESE ARE STRONG!
GRAH

DOGOOM
UGH!
GAAH!
GEH
GAH
GI
HYA
THAT THING—

SHU

DO

GYU
DON
MIRIA!
GEH
GI HYA
HYA
GI HYA?

READ THIS WAY
HYUP
BA
DA
DO
GAH
GE HEE
DO
DO
SHA
GAH
DON
GA
SHU

LOWER NUMBERS, FALL BACK!
ONLY SINGLE DIGITS WILL BEAR THE BRUNT!
ONLY THOSE CONFIDENT IN THEIR SKILLS MUST LEND SUPPORT!

READ THIS WAY

GA

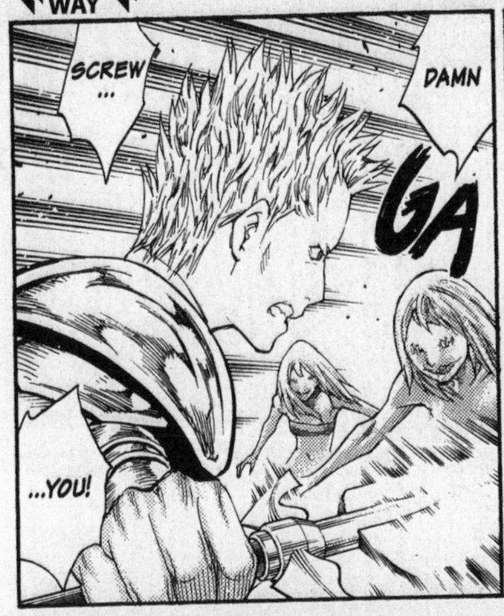
DAMN
SCREW ...
GA
...YOU!

URGH ...
GA
UNGH!
UGH!

!
ARGH ...

GA
GA

GA
GAKI

THIS IS BAD ...
THE DIF-FERENCE IN NUMBERS IS TOO GREAT...

GAAAN
GAAN
GAAAN

DAMN.
WHAT THE HELL...
...IS GOING ON?!

NO ONE FROM THE ORGANI-ZATION IS HERE IN ALL THE CONFUSION...
...SO THIS IS MY CHANCE TO ESCAPE, BUT...
!!
DOGOOOO
WHOA!

!

WHA ...
WHAT THE ...?!

クレイモア

Claymore

READ THIS WAY
BIKI
BIKI BIKI
!
DO
GA
A
AP
SCENE 115: CORPSE OF THE WITCH, PART 2

DAMN!
WHO IS THAT?!
!
CHIL-DREN ...?
THE ORGANI-ZATION'S WARRIORS IN TRAINING ...?
GO
DOGAA

FW IP
DAN
TCH!
!
SORRY ...
...BUT I'M BORROW-ING THAT.
GA S HA

GYUA
CLANK
GAA
GAA
GA
WHAK
WHAK
GAA
!
!
GA
WHAK
!!

FWUP
KCH
!
GWO
THE SAME FACE ...
TWINS?
KLANNG

GYUAA
HWIP
HYU
HYU
KRIK
KLANG

READ THIS WAY
!
A MIDAIR COLLISION ALWAYS...
...BLOWS AWAY THE LIGHTER COMBATANT!
ZUSHAAAA
KLA
KLANG
WHAK
WHAK
GYUA
NNG
TMP
TMP

HYUN
GAA
GA SHA
WHO ...
... ARE YOU?
YOU MAY HAVE HELD BACK...
...BUT STILL, FIGHTING TWO WARRIORS IS TOUGH.

BECAUSE...

GA SHA

...MY SWORDMASTER WAS SORT OF YOUR SENIOR.

?

WHAT AN INTERESTING SWORD.

IT ISN'T MARKED, AND IT'S NOT MADE TO CUT.

IT MUST BE A PRACTICE SWORD.

YOU'RE NOT IN...
...THE ORGANIZATION?

THEY IMPRISONED ME HERE.
THEY DON'T LIKE ME MUCH.

DON
!

BIRI
!
BIRI
BIRI
WHAT THE HECK IS GOING ON?
THAT, AND THE WAY YOU TWO ARE ACTING...
THERE'S SOMETHING STRANGE HAPPENING.
...

READ THIS WAY

W- WE...
!
...ARE ALL FLEEING.

WE'RE USING THE WARRIORS' REBEL-LION...
...TO ESCAPE THE ORGANI-ZATION.

THE WAR-RIORS...
...ARE REBEL-LING...

BUT IF THEY CATCH US...
...THEY'LL DO EVEN MORE HORRIBLE...
...*PAINFUL* THINGS TO US.

HEY...
!
HUH?
WELL...
...MIND IF I KEEP THIS SWORD?
GA
SHA

GYAAAAH!

WHAK

GA A

GA

GWO

GASHU
AA...
AAAAAGH!

GA GA GA

UNGH!

ARGH!

SHUN

GE HEH

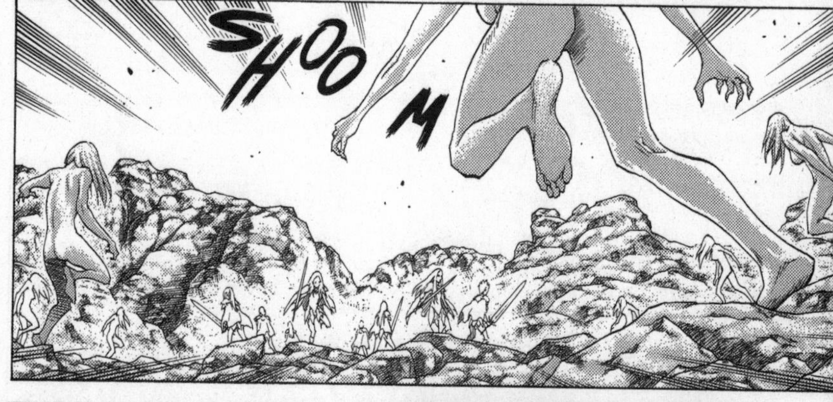

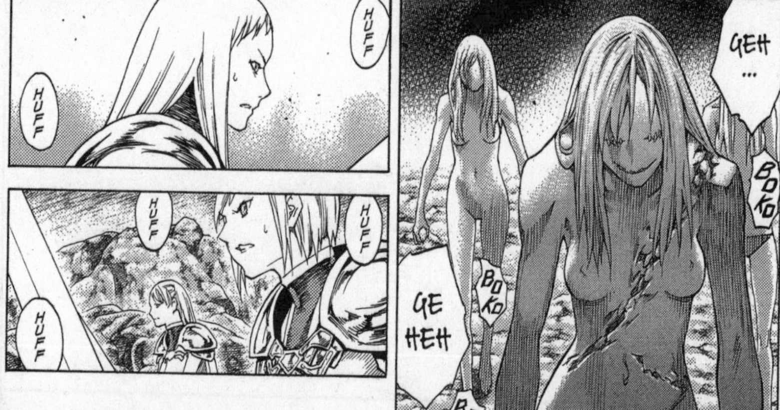

READ THIS WAY

HEY ...
...HAVE YOU NOTICED?
!

IT'S ...
... BECOMING HARDER TO KILL THEM...
...WITH ONE BLOW.

IT'S LIKELY THEY'RE LINKED, AND ARE LEARNING AS THE BATTLE PROGRESSES.
THE LONGER THIS BATTLE DRAGS ON, THE WORSE FOR US.

TMP
GRAAAH

TATMP
TCH!
DAN
!
BA
!
?!
HYUN
FWIP
FWIP
!
UH-OH!
THEY'RE GOING FOR ANYONE BUT SINGLE DIGITS!

HYU
DO
GAAA
GWO
GEH ...
!
GA
GASHU
GASHI
GAH
WHA ...

GA SHA

!

GEH
GE HEH?

WHAT'RE YOU TWO DOING HERE?
YOU WERE SUPPOSED TO DEFEND THE TRAINEES!

READ THIS WAY

ONE OF THE PRIS-ONERS ...
...TOOK OUR PLACE.

?!
A... PRIS-ONER?

A MAN WHOSE SWORDPLAY IS LIKE OURS.
HE SEEMED DIFFERENT FROM THE ORGANI-ZATION'S MEN.

BUT A SINGLE MAN...
...AGAINST THE ORGANI-ZATION'S FORCES?

DON'T WORRY.
!

IF HIS OPPO-NENTS ARE HUMAN ...
...I DOUBT HE WILL LOSE TO THEM.

GAH!
WHY YOU ...
GUH!

WHAK
WHAK
GA
GA

GA
YOU'RE MEDI-OCRE.
THEY LET OTHERS FIGHT THEIR BATTLES, AND THIS IS WHAT HAPPENS.
GA

GASHI
GAA
GA

MY SHOULDER WOUND STILL HURTS...
...BUT AGAINST YOU LOSERS, I HARDLY NOTICE!
THERE THEY ARE!
!
OVER HERE!

TUP
GET BACK HERE!
GRAB
YOU THINK YOU CAN GET AWAY IN ALL THE COMMO-TION?!
EEK!
!
DO
WHAT ...
WHY YOU ...
BA
KA
Hyun
Hyun
ARGH!

WHACK

AGH!

GAH!
GAAGH!
GAH!
DOSHA

!
!!

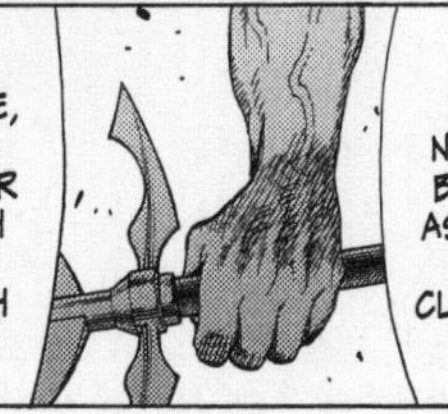
IT MAY NOT CUT, BUT IT'S AS HEAVY AS A CLAYMORE.
...

IF I STRIKE, IT'LL SUNDER FLESH AND CRUSH BONE.

GASHA
GET HIT IN THE WRONG SPOT...
...AND IT'LL BE WORSE THAN IF I HAD CUT YOU.

GA
DO DO
KA KA

TSK TSK TSK...

I THOUGHT THE ABYSS FEEDERS WOULD BE ENOUGH ...
...BUT THE TABLES HAVE TURNED.

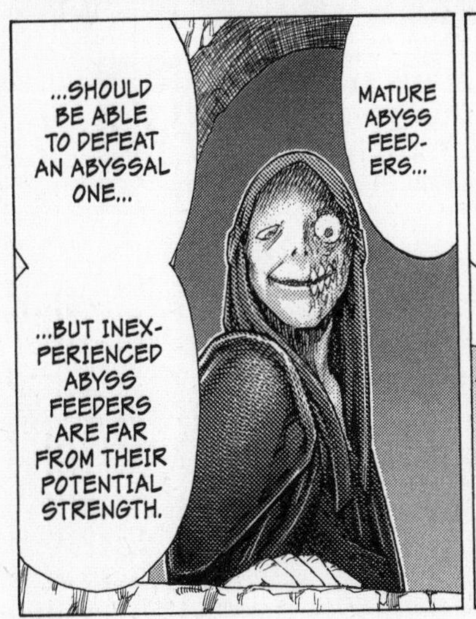
MATURE ABYSS FEED-ERS...
...SHOULD BE ABLE TO DEFEAT AN ABYSSAL ONE...
...BUT INEX-PERIENCED ABYSS FEEDERS ARE FAR FROM THEIR POTENTIAL STRENGTH.

DAE.
!
WE TOLD YOU TO MAKE HASTE.
WHAT ARE YOU DOING HERE?

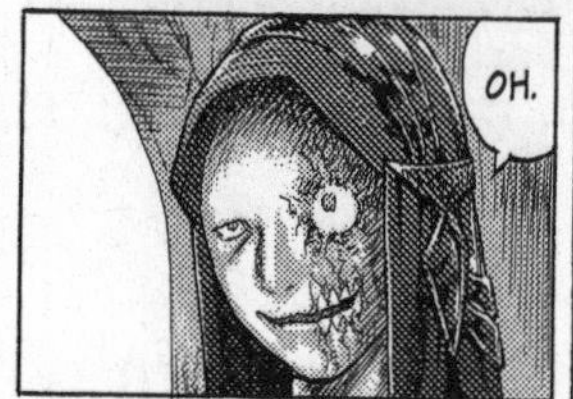
OH.

SORRY, SORRY.
I FORGOT TO INFORM YOU.
I FINISHED MY WORK AND RELEASED ALL THREE.

ARE THEY ALL...
... STABLE?

WELL, ABOUT THAT...
IT SEEMS I CHOSE THE WRONG INDIVIDUALS.

!!
WHAT ?!

READ THIS WAY

?!
WHAT ARE YOU TALKING ABOUT?

I PAID TOO MUCH ATTENTION TO STRENGTH ...
...AND FAILED TO CONSIDER THEIR ORIGINAL PERSONALITY TRAITS, LIKE OBEDIENCE.

?!

TO PUT IT BLUNTLY ...

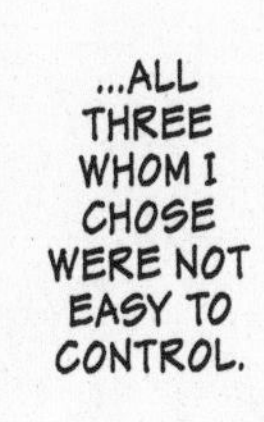
...ALL THREE WHOM I CHOSE WERE NOT EASY TO CONTROL.

D-DAE...
YOU...

THAT ISN'T TO SAY THEY WILL AWAKEN SOON.
THE DANGER WILL INCREASE WITH THE STRENGTH OF THEIR OPPONENTS.

BUT AS THEY ARE...
...THEY SHOULD PERFORM MUCH BETTER THAN NEWBORN ABYSS FEEDERS.

DENE-VE!
YEAH.
I KNOW.

GWOO

I'M GONNA PICK UP THE PACE.
ONLY FOLLOW IF YOU CAN KEEP UP.

!

DAMN!
WHAT IS THIS BIZARRE, MASSIVE YOMA ENERGY I SENSE?
IT SUDDENLY APPEARED INSIDE THE ORGANI-ZATION'S HEAD-QUARTERS.

READ THIS WAY

DAE...
...HAS NOT CHANGED.

HE DOES NOT CARE FOR THE ORGANIZATION OR THE FIGHTING IN THIS COUNTRY.
THE RESULTS OF HIS RESEARCH ARE EVERY-THING TO HIM.

BUT IT'S TOO DANGEROUS!
ORDER THEIR IMMEDIATE RETRIEVAL!

IT IS TOO LATE FOR THAT.
NOW ALL WE CAN DO IS HOPE THEY DO NOT AWAKEN.

OF THOSE WHOSE BODIES WERE COM-PLETE ...
...HE CHOSE THE STRONG-EST THREE.

HYSTERIA
THE
ELEGANT...

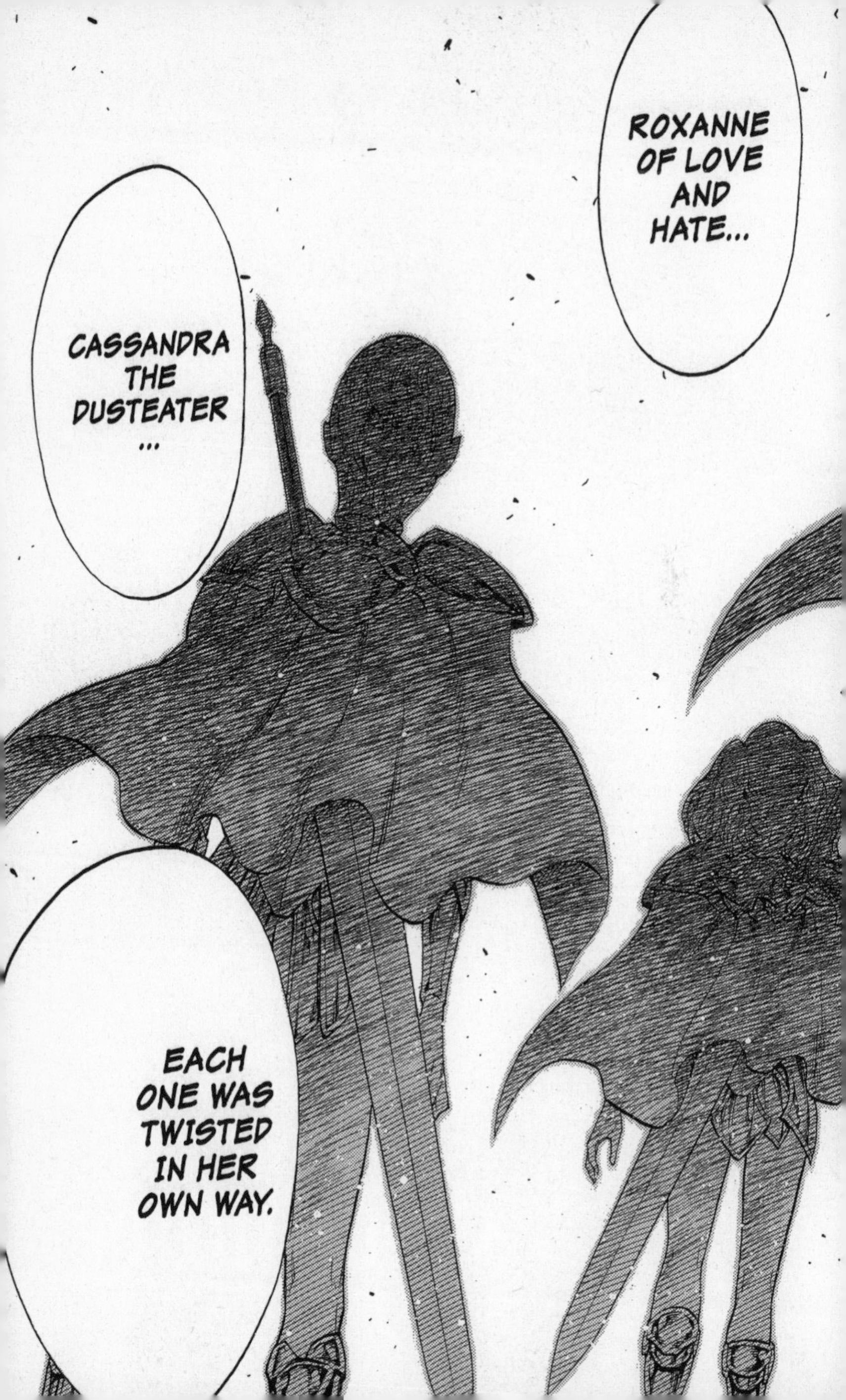
ROXANNE OF LOVE AND HATE...
CASSANDRA THE DUSTEATER...
EACH ONE WAS TWISTED IN HER OWN WAY.

クレイモア
Claymore

Scene 116: Corpse of the Witch, Part 3

THE BATTLE AGAINST THE MONSTERS THAT DIDN'T EMIT YOMA ENERGY DRAGGED ON.

PERHAPS IT WAS BECAUSE WE WERE CONCENTRATING ON OUR EYES AND EARS TOO MUCH...

...OR WAS IT BECAUSE THEY LOOKED...

...SO MUCH LIKE US?

EITHER WAY, WE WERE FATALLY LATE IN NOTICING THE APPROACH OF THE OTHERS.

Scene 116: Corpse of the Witch, Part 3

GW

!
WHAT THE...?!
GAH!
GUAH!
GAH!
GAGK!
!!

AUDREY!
RACHEL!
NINA!

!
WH-
WHO...
...ARE
YOU?!

SPLT

THE WIND CARESSING MY FACE FEELS GOOD.
IT HAS BEEN SO LONG ...

DOOM

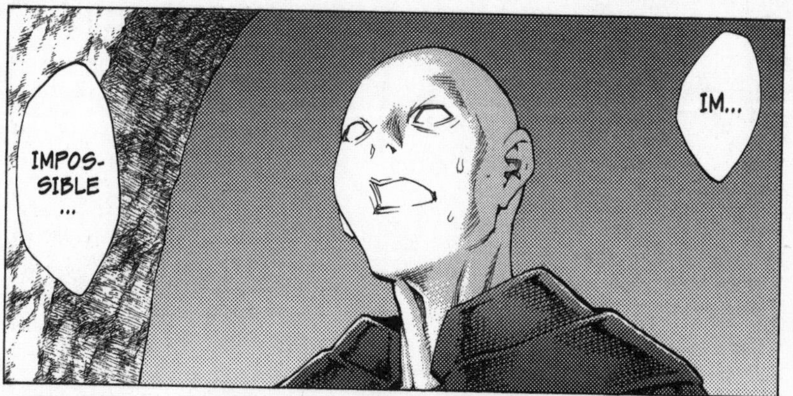
IM...
IMPOS-SIBLE...

ALL OF THEM...?
THEY ANNIHI-LATED...
...EVERY LAST ONE...
...IN SUCH A SHORT TIME?

DAE...
...YOU...
HEH HEH HEH...

DON'T TELL ME THEY ARE TOO STRONG.

I TOLD YOU AT THE START THAT I CHOSE THEM BASED ON STRENGTH.

READ THIS WAY

OOOO
?
WHAT'S THAT?
DO
MP
GW
GA
KII

READ THIS WAY
!
OH MY...
!
SHADOW CHASER.
BYUA
GAK
BA
BA
BA

GA
GAGA
GAGAA
GAA
!
!
BIKI
BIKI
GWOOO
BIKI
BIKI
BIKI
BIKI

WOO
OH
WO
GW
JUST ME AGAINST AN AWAKENED BEING...
WHAT BAD LUCK.
GIMME A BREAK.
OOO
O

KLANG
KLANG
WHAK
KLANG
WHAK
GASHA
HUFF
HUFF
HUFF
WHO IS SHE...?
THE ORGANIZATION HAS SOMEONE THIS STRONG?

READ THIS WAY

...

HEY...
...HAVE YOU HEARD OF ROCK-WELL HILL?

?
ROCK-WELL...
... HILL?

I KEEP THINKING, BUT I CAN'T SEEM TO REMEM-BER...
...MY OWN NAME.

WHAT?

IT'S LIKE THERE'S A MIST IN MY HEAD.
THE ONLY THING THAT'S CLEAR IS THAT I MUST KILL YOU ALL.

...

BUT EARLIER, WHEN THE WIND CARESSED MY CHEEKS...
...I REMEM-BERED SOME-THING.

I BELIEVE ...
...I WAS KILLED...
...AT ROCKWELL HILL.

WH...

!!

Y-YOU...
!
IMPOS-SIBLE ...

READ
THIS
WAY

HUH? WHAT IS IT?
DO YOU KNOW ME?
PLEASE, TELL ME.

...

EVERY WARRIOR KNOWS ABOUT...
...THE MASSACRE OF WARRIORS AT ROCKWELL HILL.

THE NUMBER ONE AT THE TIME REACHED THE LIMITS OF HER HUMAN HEART...
...BUT DIDN'T GIVE A BLACK CARD TO ANYONE.
ON ORDERS FROM THE ORGANIZATION, A WARRIOR FORCE WENT TO ROCK-WELL HILL TO PURGE HER.

BUT THAT NUMBER ONE WOULD NOT SUBMIT...
...AND SLAUGHT-ERED THE WARRIORS WHO SURROUNDED HER.

THEY BARELY SUCCEEDED IN TAKING HER LIFE BEFORE SHE AWAKENED...
...BUT ROCKWELL HILL WAS LITTERED WITH THE CORPSES OF THE WARRIORS WHO FOUGHT HER.

THE NAME OF THAT NUMBER ONE WAS HYSTERIA.

OF ALL THE PAST NUMBER ONES, HER FIGHTING TECHNIQUE WAS THE MOST BEAUTIFUL, AND THE MANNER OF HER DEATH THE MOST ABOMINABLE.

THAT WAS HYSTERIA THE ELEGANT!

READ THIS WAY

UH-OH...
IF IT'S TRUE...
...THEN THE OTHER TWO MAY ALSO BE DECEASED NUMBER ONES.

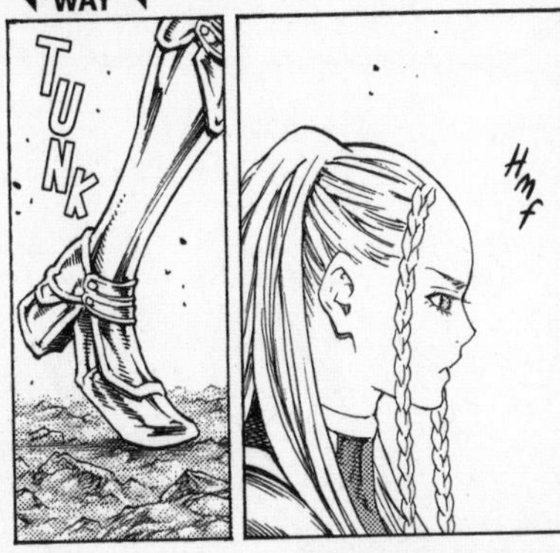
Hmf
TUNK

I...
FUWA
...HATE TO BE IGNORED.

AA...
... AAGH!
AA
BU
BU

HYUP

READ
THIS
WAY

HER FIRST STRIKE...
IT'S LIKE SHE PASSES THROUGH MY BODY.

IT TRULY IS ELEGANT ...
THE MOST BEAUTIFUL TECHNIQUE OF ANY WARRIOR...

HOW-EVER...

CLOMP

!

GASHA

THE PRINCIPLE ...
...IS MUCH LIKE THAT OF MY PHANTOM!

OH, DEAR.
MY SECOND ATTACK DIDN'T FATALLY WOUND YOU EITHER?
WHO ARE YOU?

HUFF
HUFF
HUFF

THE PRINCIPLE IS AN INSTANTANEOUS RELEASE OF YOMA POWER FOR A MOMENTARY SURGE OF SPEED.
I MAINLY USE IT TO EVADE ATTACKS AND PUT DISTANCE BETWEEN MYSELF AND MY OPPONENT...
...BUT SHE COMES FORWARD...

...AND THEN STEPS ASIDE AT THE CLOSEST PROXIMITY AND MOVES AROUND BEHIND...
...CAUSING HER AFTER-IMAGE TO APPEAR AS IF IT'S PASSING THROUGH HER OPPONENT.

IT'S EASY TO UNDERSTAND CONCEPTUALLY, BUT WHAT'S ASTOUNDING IS THE PRECISION INVOLVED.
SUPPOSING WE ARE EQUAL IN SPEED, THE ACCURACY OF HER MOVEMENT IS ON ANOTHER LEVEL.

READ THIS WAY

IT IS EXACTLY WHAT I COULD NOT ATTAIN, NO MATTER HOW I LONGED FOR IT.
AND NOW I AM CON- FRONTED WITH IT.

I AM JEALOUS ...
...OF YOUR SUPERIOR TALENT.

?

DID I KNOCK A SCREW LOOSE?
YOU'RE TRULY A STRANGE GIRL.

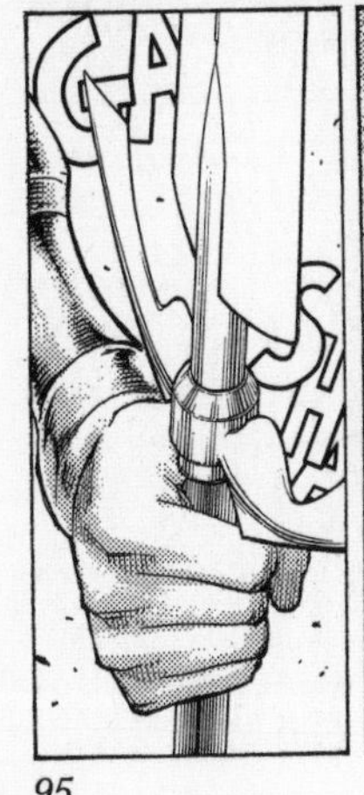

FOOM

!

BIKI
EVEN IF I LOSE IN TECHNIQUE...
BIKI
...I WILL NOT LOSE THIS FIGHT.
BIKI

BIKI
SORRY, BUT...
BIKI
...I'M SENDING YOU BACK TO THE GRAVE.
BIKI

GA
WHAK
GA
WHAK
BYUA
KI
ANG
GYUA
BYU
DOGAAA

GA
GA
GA
THIS'LL WORK ...
THE THREE OF US TOGETHER CAN BEAT HER!

URGH ...
UNGH ...
KIN
KIN
URGH ...
UGH!
UGH!
KIN

THAT FOOL.
SHE NEVER CHANGES.
KIN
KIN
GA
GA

UNGH ...
UGH...

OH, ARE YOU UP?
SHALL WE CON-TINUE, THEN?

UNGH ...
URGH ...
UGH...

HUFF
HUFF
HUFF

YOU STILL DON'T HAVE YOUR ARMS ON.
YOU CAN'T DO ANYTHING *THAT* WAY.
I'LL GIVE THEM TO YOU, SO HURRY UP AND HEAL.

READ THIS WAY

EVERY-WHERE I TURN—FOOLS.
GASHA
THE OTHER TWO DON'T EVEN REMEMBER THEIR NAMES.
BOOOR-ING.

IT WAS THE FIRST TIME I SAW THAT OTHER ONE...
...BUT YOU... YOU AND I DID FIGHT TOGETHER IN THE SAME ERA.

UGH...
UNGH.
UGH.
THEY CARVED YOU UP PRETTY BADLY, BUT I WAS THE ONE WHO FINISHED YOU OFF...
...CASSANDRA.

クレイモア

Claymore

SCENE 117: CORPSE OF THE WITCH, PART 4

ORGANIZATION WARRIOR NUMBER 35.

THAT WAS THE FIRST NUMBER ASSIGNED TO ROXANNE.

SPASHA

GA
SHA
GA
SHA

IT BEGAN WITH A MISSION TO SUBDUE A SINGLE AWAKENED BEING.
IT WAS UNUSUAL FOR ONE OF HER NUMBER TO PARTICIPATE IN THE FIGHT AS A MEMBER OF THE TEAM.

THE LEADER WAS NUMBER 5, ELIZABETH.
THE OTHERS WERE NUMBERS 18, 22 AND 31, FOR A TOTAL OF FIVE, INCLUDING ROXANNE.

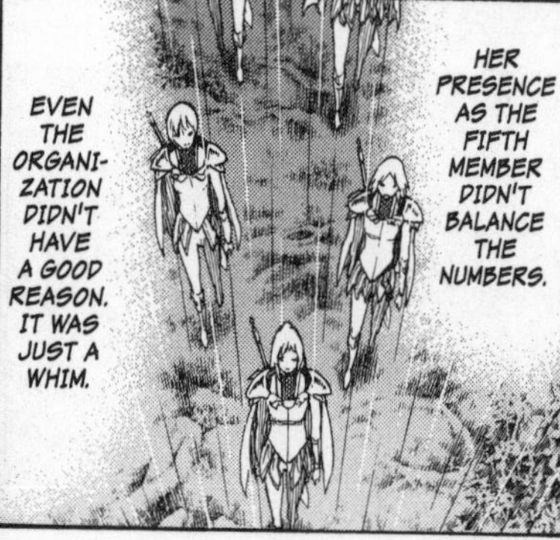
HER PRESENCE AS THE FIFTH MEMBER DIDN'T BALANCE THE NUMBERS.
EVEN THE ORGANIZATION DIDN'T HAVE A GOOD REASON. IT WAS JUST A WHIM.

READ THIS WAY

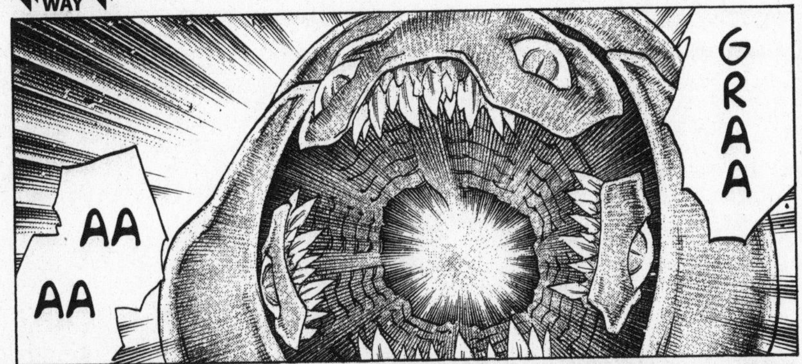
GRAA
AA
AA

UNGH ...
UNGH.

GA
GA
A
WH
AK

GA SHU
!

WH...

SO SHE BEGAN TO COPY IT.

THE AREAS THEY WERE IN CHARGE OF WERE NEAR EACH OTHER...

...BUT THEIR WAY OF FIGHTING, CONSIDERED POOR FORM BY THE OTHER WARRIORS, ISOLATED THEM AND STRENGTHENED THE BOND BETWEEN THEM.

BECAUSE OF THAT, THE TWO BECAME CLOSE.

THEN, SUDDENLY...

...ROXANNE REALIZED HER STRENGTH HAD SURPASSED THAT OF URANUS.

READ
THIS
WAY

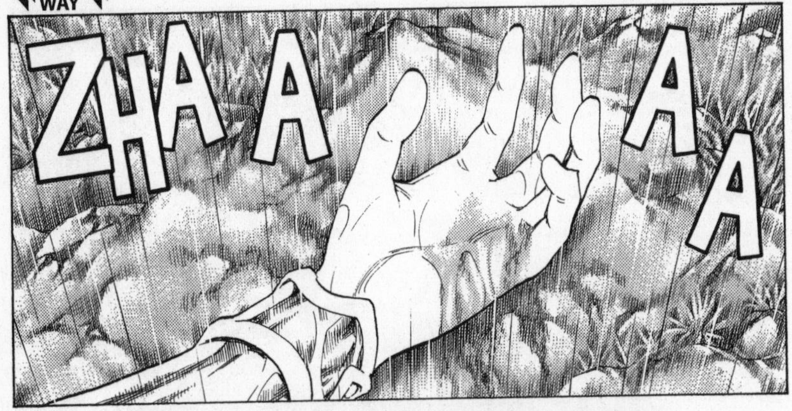
ZHAAAAA

IT WASN'T LONG BEFORE URANUS DIED...
... DIRECTLY AFTER ROXANNE WAS RAISED TO NUMBER 24.

ROX-ANNE HELPED TO SUBDUE THAT AWAK-ENED BEING...
...AND THE OTHER WARRIORS THERE REPORTED THAT NO EMOTION CROSSED HER FACE WHEN URANUS DIED.

COME ON...
GA
SHA
...KEEP UP, YOU GUYS.

NUMBER 9'S NAME WAS NADINE.
ROXANNE ADMIRED THE WAY NADINE FOUGHT WITHOUT HER RIGHT EYE, WHICH SHE HAD LOST AS A CHILD.

HER SENSE OF DISTANCE WAS POOR, SO SHE RELIED ON SENSING YOMA ENERGY WHEN SHE FOUGHT.

SO HONED WAS HER ABILITY THAT SHE COULD HAVE FOUGHT WITH HER LEFT EYE CLOSED AS WELL.

READ THIS WAY

IN THAT FIGHT...
...ROXANNE RIPPED OUT HER OWN RIGHT EYE.

NADINE WAS SUSPICIOUS...
...BUT THEY FOUGHT TOGETHER...
...AND SHE GREW TO LIKE ROXANNE, WHO HAD STUDIED HER ABILITY TO READ YOMA ENERGY IN BATTLE.

EVENTUALLY, THEY PARTICIPATED AS PARTNERS...
...IN SUBDUING SO MANY AWAKENED BEINGS THAT THE ORGANIZATION TOOK NOTICE.

NADINE DIED...
...ABOUT THE TIME ROXANNE WAS APPROACH-ING HER LEVEL OF ABILITY.

HER OPPO-NENT WAS A SINGLE LOW NUMBER'S AWAK-ENED BEING.
THE WARRIORS WHO FOUGHT WITH HER WERE SURPRISED THAT A NUMBER 9 COULD LOSE HER LIFE IN SUCH A FIGHT.

!

WHAT SUR-PRISED THEM EVEN MORE ...
...WAS THE WAY THE MOMENT NADINE DIED, ROXANNE'S RIGHT EYE RETURNED.

READ
THIS
WAY

BY THE TIME ROXANNE BECAME NUMBER 11...
...THE OTHER WARRIORS FOUND HER UNSETTLING.

ELIZABETH, NUMBER 5 AND LEADER OF THAT FIRST OUTING TO SUBDUE AN AWAKENED BEING...
...DIED SOON AFTER ROXANNE HAD STOLEN ALL HER BEAUTIFUL SWORDPLAY.

WHEN ROXANNE BECAME NUMBER 5...
...THE NUMBER 1 AT THE TIME WAS UNAPPROACH-ABLE.

HER NAME WAS CASSANDRA.

UNUSUAL FOR A WARRIOR, SHE HELD HER SWORD IN HER LEFT HAND. EVEN THE NUMBER 2 WAS FAR BENEATH HER.

SHE DIDN'T EVEN FORM TEAMS WITH ANYONE TO FIGHT AWAKENED BEINGS.

SHE WENT TO CONFRONT AWAKENED BEINGS ALONE.

WHATEVER HER OPPONENT, SHE CAME BACK WITHOUT A SINGLE SCRATCH.

ROXANNE WAS STRONGLY ATTRACTED TO CASSANDRA...

...WITH A MIXTURE OF LOVE, RESPECT AND DESIRE SUCH AS SHE'D NEVER KNOWN BEFORE.

GASHA
!

TINK
!

ROXANNE FIRST MET CASSANDRA IN THE MOUNTAINS OF LAUTREC.
WHETHER IT WAS BY CHANCE OR PREDESTINED, ROXANNE SPOKE TO HER WITHOUT HESITATING.

HARDLY ANY OF THE WARRIORS EVER SPOKE TO CASSANDRA BECAUSE SHE WAS LIKE A GODDESS TO THEM.

AT A WORD FROM ROXANNE, WHO OUT OF ADMIRATION HAD CHANGED HER SWORD HAND, SHE AVERTED HER EYES AND BLUSHED.

AND SHE HAD DEVELOPED THE UNUSUAL TECHNIQUE OF BEING ABLE TO COMPLETELY HIDE...

...HER YOMA ENERGY FROM SPECIFIC TARGETS.

GRA
GRA
GRA
GRA

GASHA

OH, WEL-COME BACK.
ANOTHER DAY OF SLAYING AWAKENED BEINGS ALL BY YOURSELF?
!

ROXANNE...
...WHAT ARE YOU...
...DOING HERE?

OH MY, CAS-SANDRA ...
... THERE'S A LITTLE DIRT ON YOUR CHEEK.

!!

READ THIS WAY

YOU'RE NUMBER 1...
...BUT YOU DON'T HAVE AN EPITHET.

!

EVEN I'M ROXANNE OF LOVE AND HATE.
WE ALL HAVE THESE SILLY NAMES.
IT'S STRANGE THAT YOU, OUR NUMBER 1, DON'T HAVE ONE.

NO ...
... IT'S ...
...NO MATTER.

BUT...
...NO ONE'S EVER SEEN YOU REALLY FIGHT, SO WE COULD ONLY BASE ONE ON HOW YOU LOOK.

READ THIS WAY

KLA
NNG
!
URGH
...

READ THIS WAY

GA

GA A

GA

SHU

GWOO

TAKE THIS!

HYUN
!
!
GASHA
HUFF
HUFF
HUFF
?
WHAT WAS THAT...?

READ THIS WAY

IF YOU HAD JUST NOT WORRIED ABOUT OTHERS SEEING AND DONE THAT FROM THE START...
...YOU COULD HAVE SPARED YOURSELF SOME INJURIES.
wobble
wobble
wobble
IT'S A BLUFF.
BA
BA
I'M FINISHING HER OFF!
W...
WAIT!
RA—
BYUN
WH
OOM

HUH?!
FWUM
P
DA
SHUU
GYAA...
...AAAH!
RACHEL!

WHY YOU...
BY
U
A
BY
U
SECRET SWORD ...
... SHADOW CHASER.
Byun
GA
SH
GAH!
GUAH!
NINA!

READ THIS WAY

SHE SWINGS HER HEAD LIKE A PENDULUM...
RIGHT ... LEFT ...

HWIP
ARGH!
GYU A

WHAT THE...
...HELL?!

THEN SHE USES THE CENTRIFUGAL FORCE TO LOWER HERSELF...
...LOWER AND LOWER...

OOO
GA
SHU
UGH!
GAAAAAH!

GWO

GWOO

MUNCHING ON MUD AND SWALLOW-ING SAND...
YOU NEVER DID LIKE FIGHTING THAT WAY.

I NAMED YOU THE DUST-EATER.
PER-FECT, DON'T YOU THINK?

NEITHER WARRIOR NOR AWAKENED BEING...
...CAN ACCURATELY STRIKE AN OBJECT...
...THAT COMES SLIDING AT THEM SUDDENLY ALONG THE GROUND.

クレイモア
Claymore

Scene 118: Corpse of the Witch, Part 5

SCENE 118: CORPSE OF THE WITCH, PART 5

READ THIS WAY

!!
UNGH!

TCH!

WHY YOU...
TUMP

GWO

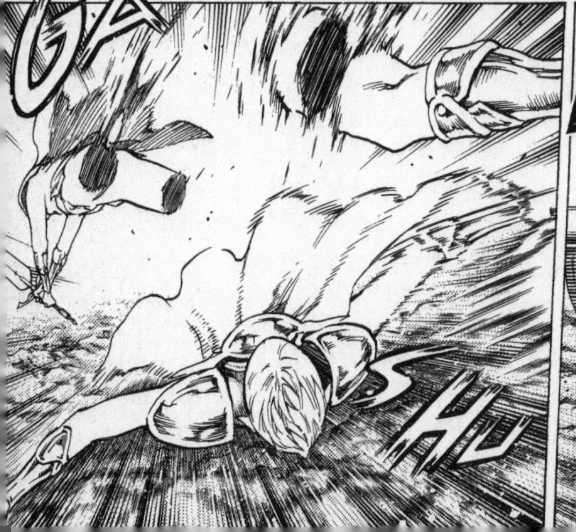
GASHU

NGH...
wobble
WHUD

HYUN

HYUN

FIRST THE LEGS ...
THEN THE ARMS ...

GON

HACK HACK
HACK
UNGGG ...
... GGHHH ...!
HYUP
GASH
DO GA A
FWOON
DO GA GA

SHE CREEPS ALONG THE GROUND, SCRAPING HER FACE ACROSS THE SURFACE...
...AND COMPLETELY BLOCKS HER ENEMIES FROM MOVING BEFORE FINISHING THEM OFF.
OF ALL THE NUMBER ONES, HER WAY OF FIGHTING IS THE UGLIEST AND CRUELEST.
I HAD NO USE FOR A TECHNIQUE ...
...THAT I WOULDN'T WANT OTHER WARRIORS TO SEE.
RUB
RUB
RUB
RUB
HUFF
HUFF
HUFF
GASHA
!
SWIP

READ THIS WAY
HUFF
HUFF
HUFF
WHAT AN...
...AWFUL WAY TO DIE.
GA
SHU
AUDREY!

HUFF
HUFF
HUFF

!

!

HUFF
HUFF
HUFF

HUH?

HER STRIKE WAS DIVERTED?
THE TRAJECTORY OF THE SWORD WAS SLIGHTLY REROUTED.

READ
THIS
WAY

IT SEEMS ...
...THERE'S SOMEONE STRANGE JUST OVER THERE.

DOGAAP

DOSHAA

HUFF
HUFF
WHEW ...

HEY, ARE YOU ALL RIGHT?
WHY WERE THESE GUYS HOLDING A WARRIOR?

HUFF
HUFF
HUFF
drip
drip
drip

!
SHUNK
SHUNK
SHUNK
SHUNK
SHUNK
SHUNK
?
SHUNK
?
SHUNK
?
SHUNK

HEY, YOU—
SORRY, BUT...

...JUST...
...LET ME DO THIS.

?!

TO ME, THE WARRIORS WERE NOT COMRADES.
ONLY ONE WARRIOR IN THE ORGANI-ZATION WAS TRAINED TO FIGHT AGAINST WARRIORS.
THAT WAS ME.

I HAD NO CLASS-MATES AND NO FRIENDS.
THEY SIMPLY GAVE ME THE NUMBER 10.
I AM TOTALLY DIFFERENT FROM THE OTHER WARRIORS.

I WAS SO JEALOUS THAT TIME...
...WHEN THE WARRIORS ALL BANDED TOGETHER WITH ONE WILL.

READ THIS WAY

NONE OF US FIGHT FOR THE ORGANI-ZATION.
BUT ON OUR DEAD-END PATH...

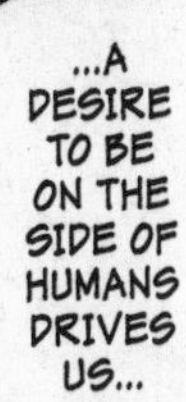
...A DESIRE TO BE ON THE SIDE OF HUMANS DRIVES US...
...AND WE FIGHT FOR OUR LOST FAMILY AND FRIENDS.

AND WE HOPE TO FIGHT FOR THE WARRIORS ...
...WHO LIVE AND FIGHT AT OUR SIDE.

SO HERE AT THE END...
...LET ME BE THEIR COMRADE.

SWIP

THERE!
THIS WAY!
GASHA
GASHA

GU
AA
CLOMP
ARGH! YOU!
IF YOU HAD KILLED US EARLIER, THEN—

GA
K

ARGH ...
WHY YOU...

DO
GA

!
WHAT THE...

READ THIS WAY

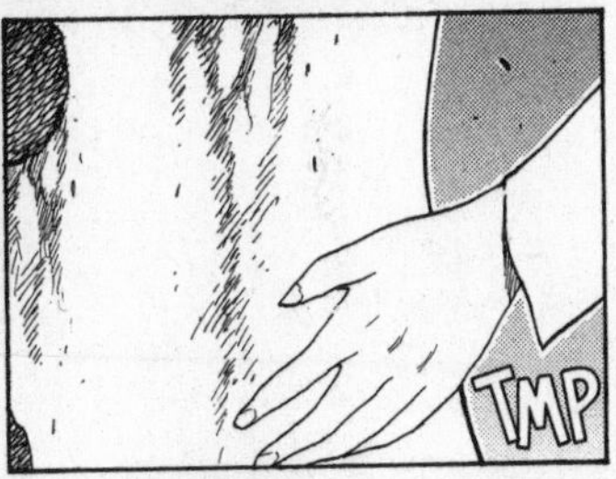

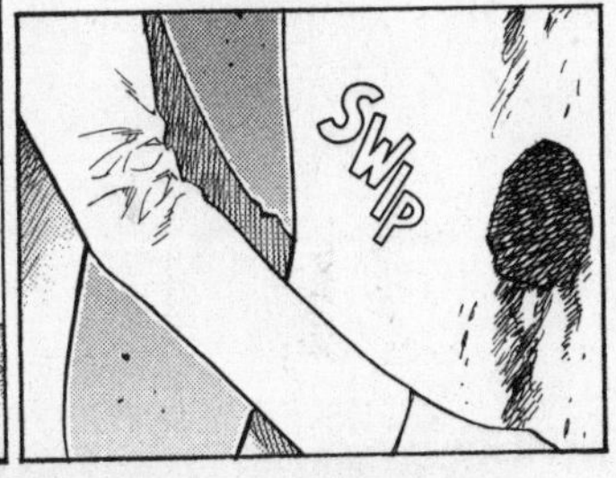

I DON'T GET IT, BUT IF THAT'S WHAT YOU HAVE TO DO...
...THEN LET THESE LITTLE TYKES SUPPORT YOU.

GASHA
GASHA

WHILE YOU DO...
GASHA
...I'LL BRING DOWN SOME MAYHEM ON THESE GUYS FOR YOU.

KLANG
DOGAAA

READ THIS WAY

TSK ...
... TSK ...
... TSK.
WHAT HAP-PENED?

SUDDENLY YOUR MOVEMENT'S NOT SO GREAT.
ARE YOU *TIRED* ALREADY?

OR ARE YOU BOTH-ERED BY...
...THE DECREASE OF YOUR COMRADES' YOMA ENERGY?
HUFF
HUFF
HUFF
GA SHA

GASHA
KRUMBL
KRUMBL

SHE IS TRULY STRONG ...
HUFF
I CAN'T WIN IF I'M WORRYING ABOUT THE OTHERS.
HUFF
HUFF

DON
!

BIKI
BIKI
BIKI

GIVE IT UP, WOULD YOU?
EVEN IF YOU RELEASE YOMA ENERGY, YOU CAN'T KEEP UP WITH MY SPEED.
YOU JUST KEEP PLOWING INTO ME. TO BE HONEST, IT'S BORING.

READ THIS WAY

BIKI
BIKI
BIKI
BIKI

I HAD...
...AN IDEA EARLIER.
DO
N
HYUN
HERE WE GO AGAIN...
GA

GA GA
KLANG
KLANG
WHAK
WSH
HYUN
WHUP
WHUP
KLANG

READ THIS WAY
HYUN
HYUN
HYUN
WHSH
WHSH
WHSH
BYU
WHSH
GO...
WHSH
HMPH.
HYUA

ZUBAAAA

!!

IT STARTED WHEN OPHELIA'S ACTION CAUSED HILDA TO AWAKEN.

I LOST MYSELF AND FOR A MOMENT SURPASSED MY LIMITS OF YOMA POWER RELEASE.

YOU JUST NARROWLY AVOID FATAL INJURIES...
KANG
KANG
...BUT YOU'RE GOOD.
WHAK
WHAK
WHAK

FOR MY PHANTOM TECHNIQUE, I RAISE MY YOMA ENERGY FOR AN INSTANT TO GO FROM A NORMAL STATE TO MY YOMA POWER RELEASE LIMIT.
SO FOR A TECHNIQUE TO SURPASS THE PHANTOM, I WOULD MOMENTARILY RAISE MY YOMA ENERGY FROM A STATE OF YOMA POWER RELEASE TO BEYOND MY LIMIT.

IT DOESN'T HAVE A FRAGMENT OF HYSTERIA'S ELEGANT ACCURACY ...
...BUT IT IS A SIMPLE AND COARSE TECH-NIQUE THAT MAXI-MIZES SPEED.
YOU COULD SAY...
...I AWAKEN FOR A MOMENT.
IT IS AN INCREDIBLY DANGEROUS METHOD.

HYUA
ZUBAA
YOU'LL ...
...REACH YOUR LIMIT SOON.
UNGH ...
GUAH!

I WON'T MAKE THAT MISTAKE AGAIN.

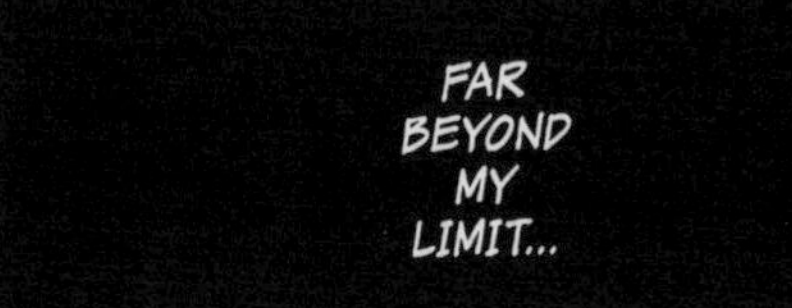

GW

WHA...

DO GA
A
A

Y...
YOU
...

ZUBAAAA

SHALL WE BEGIN?
NOW WE START TRIMMING AWAY EACH OTHER'S LIFE.

...

ARE YOU...
... CRAZY?

クレイモア
Claymore

GY

DOA

SCENE 119: CORPSE OF THE WITCH, PART 6

ARGH! IS SHE CRAZY?!
SUCH A HAP-HAZARD MOVE...

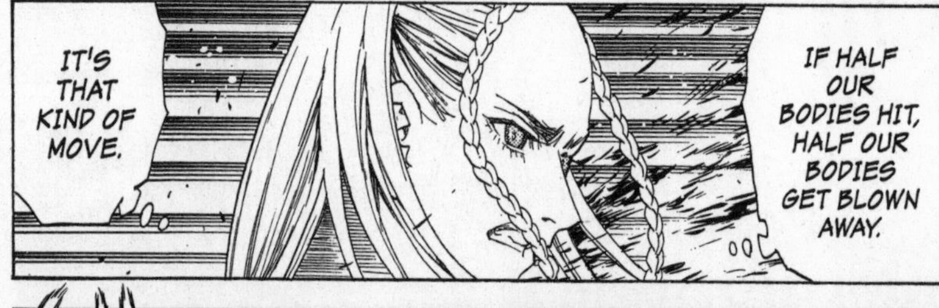
IF HALF OUR BODIES HIT, HALF OUR BODIES GET BLOWN AWAY.
IT'S THAT KIND OF MOVE.

GWO
GU
...
UNGH!

GA
SSHU

ZU
BA
A

WHO INFLICTS MORE DAMAGE IS PRACTICALLY UP TO CHANCE...
IT ISN'T TECH-NIQUE SO MUCH AS SUICIDE!

IT'S AN AWFUL WAY TO FIGHT.
IT'S UGLY AND IT MAKES ME WANT TO VOMIT ...

FROM ONE WHO HAS THE MOST ELEGANT TECH-NIQUE...
...THAT IS AN HONOR.

TCH.

OH MY...
...THERE YOU ARE. WHAT A DIRTY FIGHT.

THE RESUR-RECTED WARRIORS WERE FIGHTING SO PRETTILY ...
...BUT NOW IT'S LIKE THEY'VE BEEN DRAGGED DOWN INTO THE MUD.

AND ...
...AS FOR ME...

READ THIS WAY

HUFF
HUFF
HUFF
HUFF

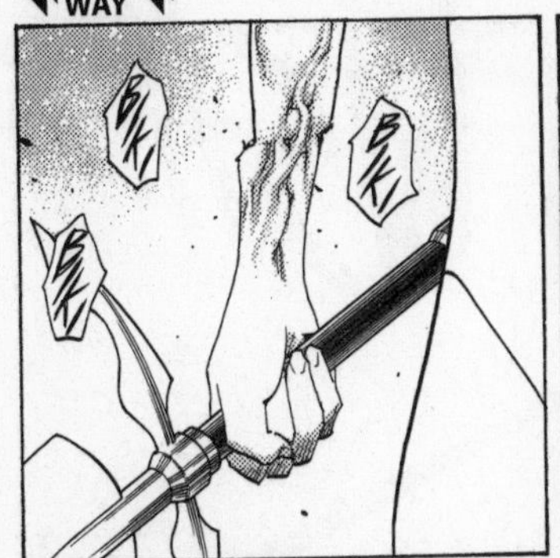
BIKI
BIKI
BIKI

WHAT'S THAT?
I WAITED ALL THIS TIME, AND YOU'RE HARDLY BACK TOGETHER AT ALL!

IF YOU USE TOO MUCH POWER TO FIGHT AT THE VERY BEGINNING, YOU WON'T HAVE ANY YOMA ENERGY LEFT FOR HEALING.
THAT'S WHY I HATE FIGHTING CHILDREN.

HUFF
HUFF
HUFF

I THOUGHT THIS MIGHT BE A *LITTLE BIT* FUN...
BUT I GUESS NOT.

OH WELL.
IT'S TIME YOU DIED.

WSH

KLANG
GAAAAAH!
YOU CAN STILL FIGHT ONCE YOU GET IN THE MOOD!
OH...
KLANG
KLANG
AGH!
GA
AGH!
KLANG
AGH!
GA
?!
!
!
BUT YOU'RE ...
SH
AK
SHOOM
...A LITTLE TOO LATE.

ZUBABAP
SO IT GOES.
ALL DONE.
!
...
UNGH ...
UNGH ...
...NGH ...

READ THIS WAY

HM?
IT... MISSED?

WHOO
URGH ...

GA
K

HWOOM

THAT'S WEIRD.
KLANG
KLANG

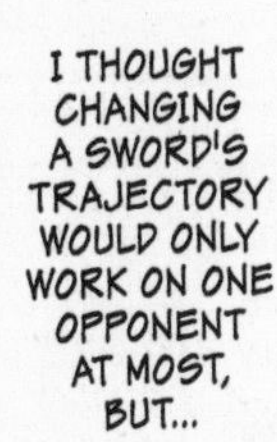
I THOUGHT CHANGING A SWORD'S TRAJECTORY WOULD ONLY WORK ON ONE OPPONENT AT MOST, BUT...

THAT MUST MEAN ...

TCH.

KLANG
KLANG
WHAT IS SHE DOING?
SHE'S NEVER BEEN ANY USE.
GA

KLANG
AND WITH MY SWORD PATH AND EYESIGHT MESSED WITH...
...THESE TWO OPPONENTS ARE PROVING TO BE A PAIN.
KLANG
GA

HUFF
HUFF
HUFF

WHAT ...?
WHAT AM I DOING?

!

A WAR-RIOR ...
WHY AM I FIGHT-ING...
...A WAR-RIOR?

BIKI
!
UNGH!

M...MY BODY ...
IT HURTS...

THEY CUT ME DOWN ...
MANY ...
...OF MY COMRADE WARRIORS ...

...
WHA ...
WHAT?

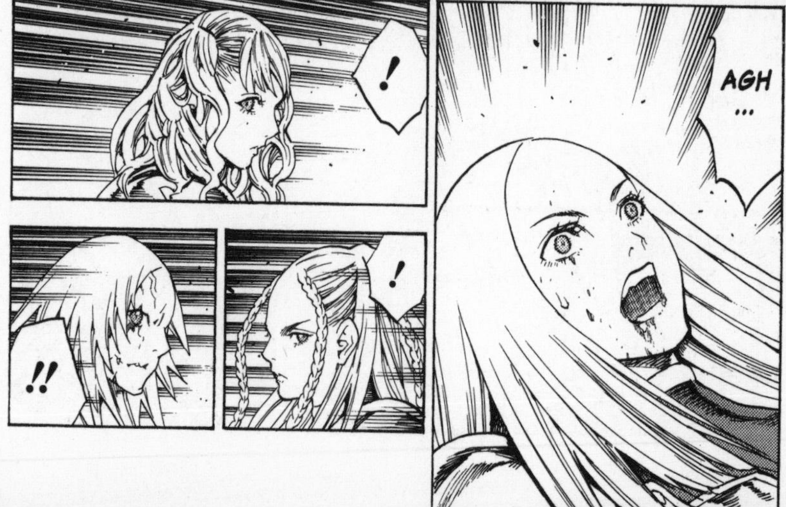
AGH ...
!
!
!!

READ
THIS
WAY

C...
CUTS
...
BIKI
BIKI
BIKI
ALL OVER MY BODY ...
WOUNDS FROM THEIR ATTACKS ...

IT HURTS!
HURTS!
HURTS!
HURTS!
HURTS!
HURTS!

WHA- WHAT THE...
SPLUT
SPLUT
SPLUT
WHAT THE HELL IS GOING ON?
...
AUDREY!
HM?

THE BLOWS OF MANY OF MY COMRADES FELL ON MY BODY.

THEIR FACES WERE TWISTED WITH FEAR.

I VOWED NEVER TO REVEAL THAT TECHNIQUE TO OTHERS AGAIN.

EVEN THE NUMBER 5 WHO HAD SPOKEN TO ME OUT OF ADMIRATION GAVE ME THE NAME DUSTEATER AND LEFT.

ONCE I ACCIDENTALLY USED THAT TECHNIQUE IN FRONT OF A LOWER NUMBER.

SHE WAS THE ONLY SURVIVOR OF A FAILED MISSION TO SUBDUE AN AWAKENED BEING.

SHE WEPT AND CLUNG TO ME...
...AND THANKED ME OVER AND OVER.

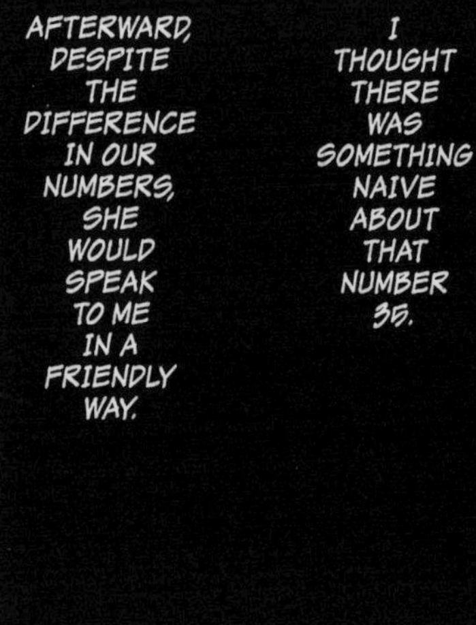
I THOUGHT THERE WAS SOMETHING NAIVE ABOUT THAT NUMBER 35.
AFTERWARD, DESPITE THE DIFFERENCE IN OUR NUMBERS, SHE WOULD SPEAK TO ME IN A FRIENDLY WAY.

I THOUGHT IT WAS STRANGE AND ASKED HER ABOUT IT ONE DAY.

SHE CASUALLY SAID THAT SHE FELT AFFECTION FOR ME BECAUSE THE WAY I RUBBED DIRT OFF MY FACE AFTER THE FIGHT WAS JUST LIKE THE WAY THE CAT AT HER HOUSE CLEANED ITSELF.

FROM THAT TIME ON, WE WERE TRUE FRIENDS.

ONE DAY, SHE WENT OUT TO SUBDUE AN AWAKENED BEING.

THE LEADER WAS NUMBER 2, ROXANNE.

A VAGUE UNEASE GRIPPED ME.

AN UNIDENTIFIABLE FRETFULNESS WELLED UP WITHIN MY BREAST.

I PRAYED FROM THE BOTTOM OF MY HEART THAT SHE WOULD COMPLETE THE MISSION AND COME BACK SAFELY.

READ THIS WAY

MY UNEASE WAS JUSTIFIED.
THE AWAKENED BEING TOYED WITH HER.
IT INFLICTED VARIOUS DEGRADATIONS ON HER AND PLUCKED OFF HER ARMS AND LEGS.
IN THE END, THE AWAKENED BEING PLAYED AROUND WITH HER SEVERED HEAD.
IT WAS ROXANNE'S FIRST FAILURE TO SUBDUE AN AWAKENED BEING.
BUT THE THREE SURVIVORS, INCLUDING ROXANNE, WERE NOT EVEN SCRATCHED.

GA SHA

OH DEAR ...
...WHAT'S THAT?

THE HEAD OF THE AWAKENED BEING YOU FAILED TO KILL.
DON'T TELL ME YOU FORGOT.

OH, DID THAT HAP-PEN?
I'VE GONE TO SUBDUE SO MANY, I JUST DON'T REMEMBER.

IT WAS AN INCREDIBLY WEAK AWAKENED BEING...

A NUMBER 2 LIKE YOU COULDN'T FAIL TO DEFEAT IT.

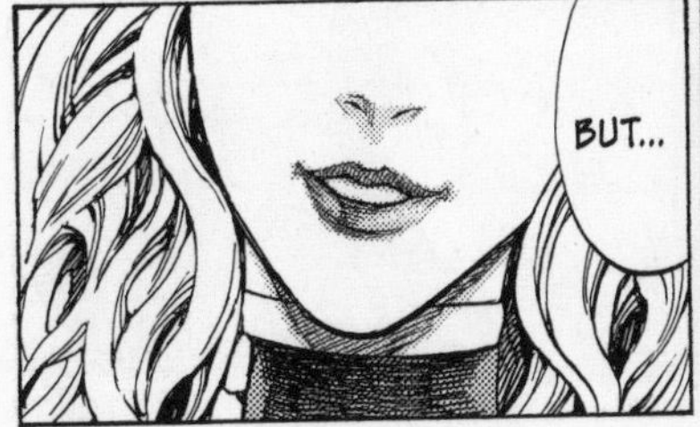

... PARTWAY THROUGH ...

...SHE STARTED LOOKING LIKE SHE WAS REALLY ENJOYING IT...

...SO I DIDN'T WANT TO INTERFERE.

I FORGOT MYSELF.

I DREW MY SWORD, AND FOR THE FIRST TIME IN A GROUP, I USED THE TECHNIQUE THAT EARNED ME THE NAME DUSTEATER.

WOULD YOU LOOK AT THAT TECH-NIQUE?
WHAT THE HELL, RIGHT?
SO UNSIGHTLY AND PATHETIC!
LAUGHABLE, RIGHT?

READ THIS WAY

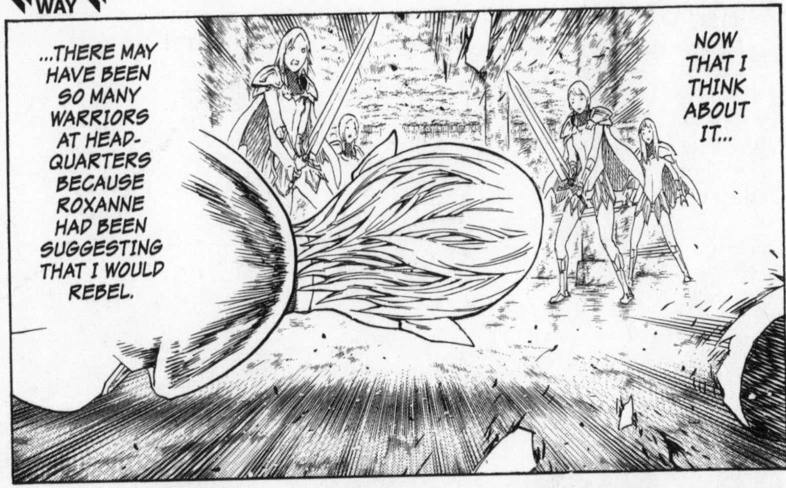
NOW THAT I THINK ABOUT IT...
...THERE MAY HAVE BEEN SO MANY WARRIORS AT HEAD-QUARTERS BECAUSE ROXANNE HAD BEEN SUGGESTING THAT I WOULD REBEL.

THEIR FACES FROZE...
...BUT THEY DIDN'T HESITATE TO DRAW THEIR SWORDS AND ATTACK.

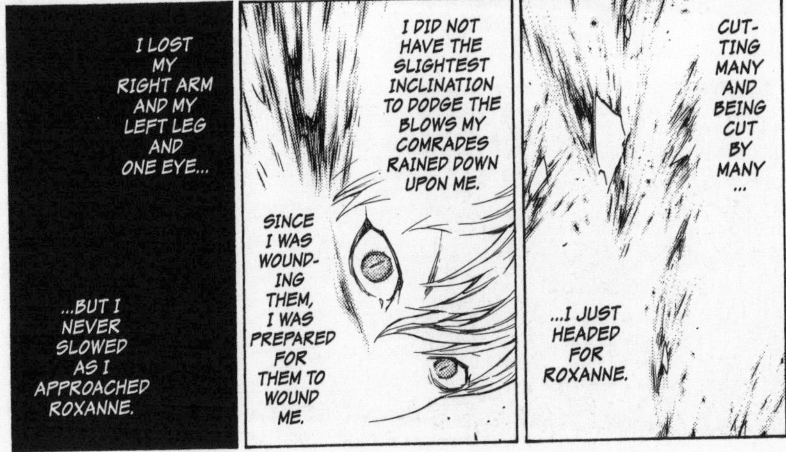
CUT-TING MANY AND BEING CUT BY MANY ...
...I JUST HEADED FOR ROXANNE.
I DID NOT HAVE THE SLIGHTEST INCLINATION TO DODGE THE BLOWS MY COMRADES RAINED DOWN UPON ME.
SINCE I WAS WOUND-ING THEM, I WAS PREPARED FOR THEM TO WOUND ME.
I LOST MY RIGHT ARM AND MY LEFT LEG AND ONE EYE...
...BUT I NEVER SLOWED AS I APPROACHED ROXANNE.

WHAT STOPPED ME AS I CRAWLED ALONG THE EARTH...

...WASN'T A BLADE, BUT THE SHARP HAFT OF A SWORD.

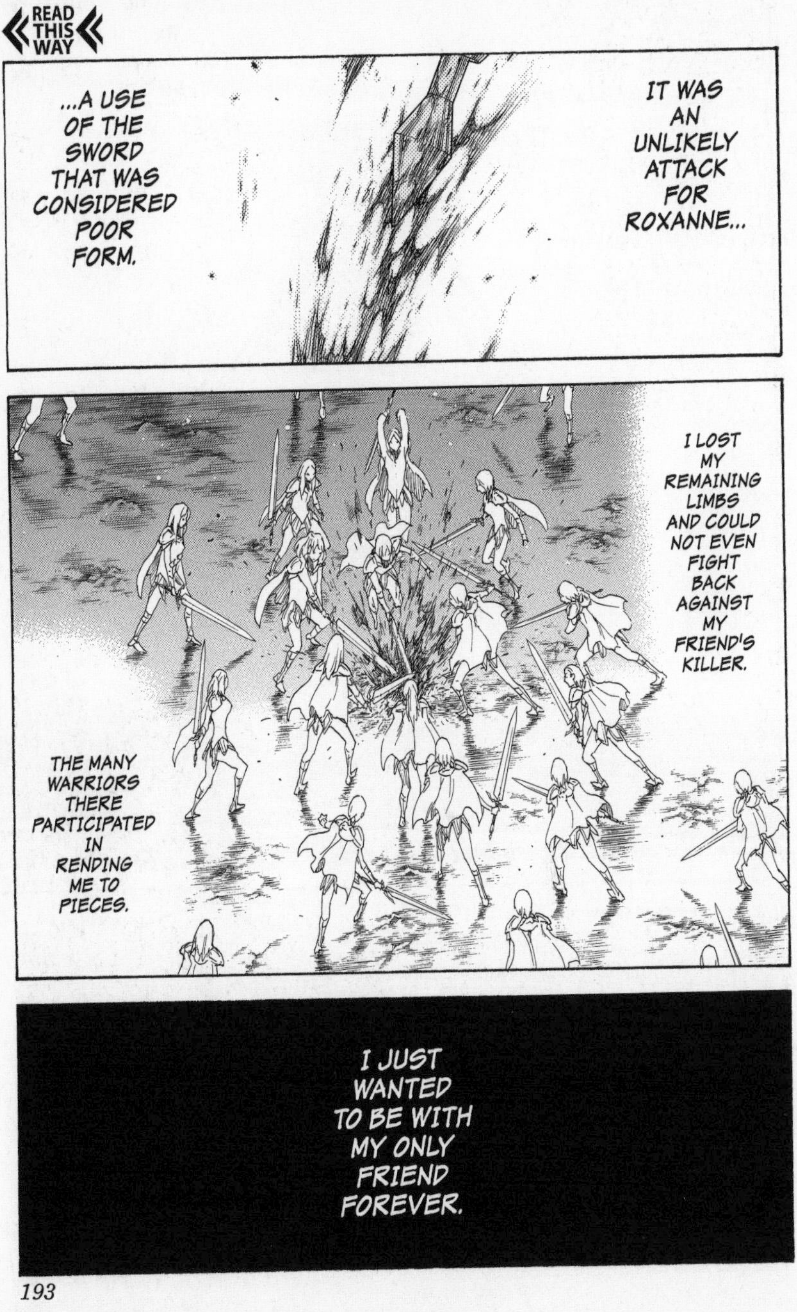

IT WAS AN UNLIKELY ATTACK FOR ROXANNE...

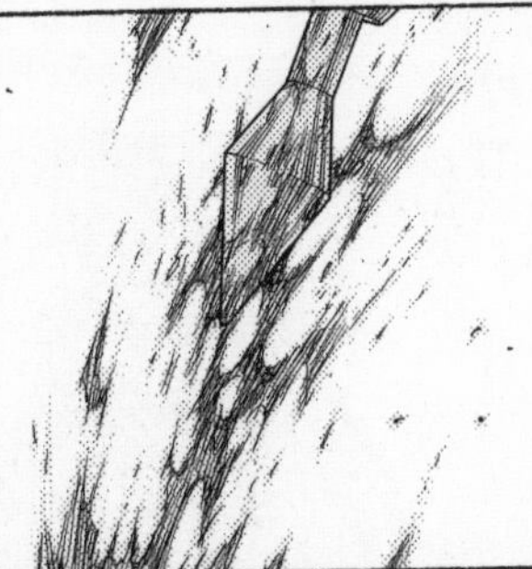

...A USE OF THE SWORD THAT WAS CONSIDERED POOR FORM.

I LOST MY REMAINING LIMBS AND COULD NOT EVEN FIGHT BACK AGAINST MY FRIEND'S KILLER.

THE MANY WARRIORS THERE PARTICIPATED IN RENDING ME TO PIECES.

I JUST WANTED TO BE WITH MY ONLY FRIEND FOREVER.

RO...
...X...
...A...
...NNE...

READ THIS WAY

OH DEAR ...
...YOU REMEMBERED.

BIKI
BIKI
BIKI

!
WHAT IS THIS ...
... MASSIVE INCREASE OF YOMA ENERGY?
BRI
BRI
BRI
BIKI
BIKI
BIKI
BIKI

THE ...
... FIRST ONE...

BO
END OF VOL. 21: CORPSE OF THE WITCH

クレイモア
Claymore

You're Reading in the Wrong Direction!!

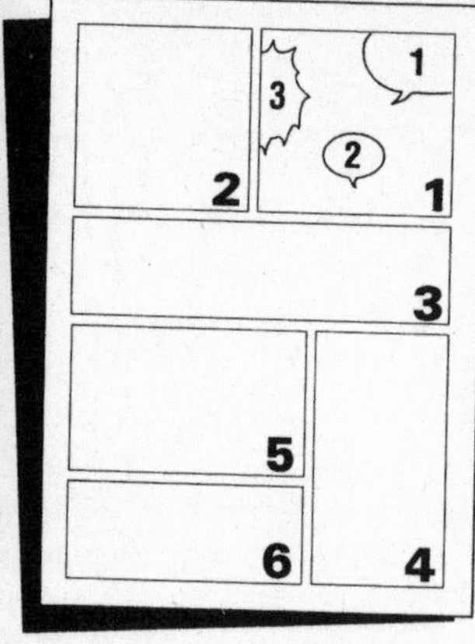

Whoops! Guess what? You're starting at the wrong end of the comic!

...It's true! In keeping with the original Japanese format, **Claymore** is meant to be read from right to left, starting in the upper-right corner.

Unlike English, which is read from left to right, Japanese is read from right to left, meaning that action, sound effects and word-balloon order are completely reversed... something which can make readers unfamiliar with Japanese feel pretty backwards themselves. For this reason, manga or Japanese comics published in the U.S. in English have sometimes been published "flopped"—that is, printed in exact reverse order, as though seen from the other side of a mirror.

By flopping pages, U.S. publishers can avoid confusing readers, but the compromise is not without its downside. For one thing, a character in a flopped manga series who once wore in the original Japanese version a T-shirt emblazoned with "M A Y" (as in "the merry month of") now wears one which reads "Y A M"! Additionally, many manga creators in Japan are themselves unhappy with the process, as some feel the mirror-imaging of their art skews their original intentions.

We are proud to bring you Norihiro Yagi's **Claymore** in the original unflopped format. For now, though, turn to the other side of the book and let the adventure begin...!

—Editor